WELFARE BECAME MY
Stepping Stone

Gladys Delores Goins

Author's Tranquility Press
ATLANTA, GEORGIA

Copyright © 2024 by Gladys Delores Goins

All rights reserved. No part of this publication may be reproduced, distributed or transmitted in any form or by any means, including photocopying, recording, or other electronic or mechanical methods, without the prior written permission of the publisher, except in the case of brief quotations embodied in critical reviews and certain other noncommercial uses permitted by copyright law. For permission requests, write to the publisher, addressed "Attention: Permissions Coordinator," at the address below.

Gladys Delores Goins/Author's Tranquility Press
3900 N Commerce Dr. Suite 300 #1255
Atlanta, GA 30344, USA
www.authorstranquilitypress.com

Ordering Information:
Quantity sales. Special discounts are available on quantity purchases by corporations, associations, and others. For details, contact the "Special Sales Department" at the address above.

Welfare Became My Stepping Stone / Gladys Delores Goins
Paperback: 978-1-964362-50-2
eBook: 978-1-964362-44-1

Contents

Introduction i

Early Childhood To Adult Life 1

From Welfare To Prosperity 15

My Identity, How I See Myself Today 22

What Is Welfare/Afdc 24

Breaking The Generational Curse Of Welfare 25

My Vision For Women 32

Personal Expression 33

I Will Rise From Where I Am 34

Principal Keys For Daily Living 38

What If I Had Stayed Connected To
The Welfare System 43

Today, This Is My Life 47

Identified With The Word Of God 49

Introduction

This is a story to honor a young woman who faced the abandonment of her husband, leaving her with two children while pregnant with her third child, with no money, limited work skills, and three children to provide for. She called on all the help she could get. With her faith in God, encouragement, and help from her family, she faced the situation. She swallowed her pride and applied for welfare. She vowed welfare would be her stepping stone, an open door to a better life for her and her children. And it was! After her baby was born, she attended school in order to become a Licensed Practical Nurse. She found a good-paying job and a whole lot of self-respect. She shares her ups and downs in her stories, giving advice and spiritual strength, especially to those women who are presently receiving government assistance. Her message is: I did it and you can too! Let welfare become your stepping stone to a better life!

Early Childhood To Adult Life

As a child, I grew up in the rural area of Richmond. My parents were common laborers doing farming and domestic work. My family was quite large, with five sisters and seven brothers, mom and dad, so I was always busy and never lonely.

I enjoyed things of a normal childhood, including dolls, rings around the roses, hopscotch, dancing, singing, and reciting. At age five, I discovered that I could sing and made my way to the step ladder every day and sang to the Lord. While singing every song, I could feel the presence of God, not knowing exactly what was happening, but it was different. Fear never came upon me. Every day my family would be inside the house. After a while, they would call out to me, "Mia, it's getting dark outside; it's time to come inside for supper!" Being at the foot of the step ladder was a peaceful place. I never wanted to leave. Elementary school at Peterson Elementary was ok. The children were much like me, growing up on the farm, but we all had something different to share.

I joined the marching band in the Third Grade and remained in the band.

I would work every evening after school on the farm from June to September (the summer months). I would think, this is so awful; I wanted to get a job and work like other kids. There were always mom's objections to my working on a public job until I was eighteen years old. All through the years of my growing up, I could only attend church and school. My sisters and brothers hardly ever played with other children outside of school. I was always active in school, singing, dancing, speaking, dramas, and acting.

I was very popular at school as a senior. The guys liked me but would talk about me so terribly when I refused to go to the extreme of being intimate. They would call me the "Big Virgin." Mom would always say, "Mia, don't isolate yourself with boys. If you do, then you have no defense. They will want to touch and fondle you. Just keep your distance from them." At the time I was seventeen years old. Mom always taught me and my sisters that a woman or a girl doesn't have to go to bed with a guy to prove anything. One of my mom's favorite sayings was "If you start having sex before marriage, you are asking for it. You will either become pregnant or contract a venereal disease. Then what?! In most cases, he won't be the man that will marry you anyway. All men will be men, children. One day you will see and understand what I am telling you. I know there are some fellows who want to get close to you; don't let them swell your head with their saying that you are so fine and pretty, which is a fact. You are a beautiful young lady who has everything going for herself. You know it's your senior year in high school. Who is taking you to the prom? If the guy drinks and smokes, he will not be taking you. Your brother will take you or you won't go to the prom." I had worked very hard. No one really met Mom's expectations. My brother Franklin took me to the prom. The next week was awards day and graduation. I received awards in music, speech, and drama, and the best all-around girl medal.

I had already made plans to attend college, when my dad was laid off from work, leaving only my mom working for a while. My younger sister and I started to work at St. Benedict Hospital in the Dietary Dept. to help get money for our home which was being remodeled during this same time. Dad worked for a short time in a plant and paper mill. The younger brother and sister did the farm work while we helped my older sisters who were in college and beauty school. We managed. At age nineteen, I debuted to society sponsored by a sorority. I entered the talent competitions and placed second for Ms. Fashionette. My oldest brother, who was just home from the U.S. Army, escorted me in the cotillion. My sister and my prospective brother-in-law stood for Mom and Dad. They felt it was too much against the Christian Standard for us to be at a dance. I understood because they were strong, strict, disciplinarian, devoted and devout Christians. This was the way they had reared us.

Shortly after this time, I got ill and had to undergo surgery. I stayed in St. Benedict Hospital, where I worked for a total of eighteen months. As I recovered from major surgery in October 1965, I was twenty years old. That summer of the same year, I started enrolling in various colleges to become a Barber. I moved to Los Angeles in May of 1966 to live with Aunt and Uncle Smitty. They were sort of like mom and dad, strict on me.

Oh, I was so thrilled to learn from my cousin Jennifer that my high school boyfriend Greg was that close to my Aunt Minnie. We found each other and started seeing each other whenever he would come to LA from Long Beach on weekends. Uncle and Aunt gave him their house rules, my curfew time and what they expected. Greg was always very smart in school but played a lot. Now I could see that he had grown up a lot. I would enjoy going to Sigma Hills and looking out over California, going to see friends just for fun, all but the partying and drinking. It took me some time to adjust to this. I would swap glasses or drink cokes and water. I just couldn't drink or smoke. Greg and I continued dating until he went overseas with the U.S. Navy. We kept in touch. He had asked me to marry him. So I wrote home and told Mom and Dad. I went to Barber School for six months, but when Greg left for overseas, things were not the same. I enjoyed associating with my classmates at school, but it wasn't the same without Greg. I wrote and told Mom that I was coming home in October. She said OK. Mom was still a little in shock about Greg and I getting married after his discharge from the Navy in November.

We set the wedding date for December 10, 1966, mom still a bit on edge. I felt she never really liked Greg because of the kind of family background he had. His dad wasn't really a family man. Greg's grandmother and mother were the strongest in his life. His father didn't attend church either. Greg and I weren't strangers to each other. It had only been three years since finishing high school at the same school. Nothing I said seemed to matter to Mom. She kept focusing on the fact that she felt he was not of a good standard of living. She asked, "Do you think he will provide for you and your children if you decide to rear a family?" I said, "Yes, mom!" She said, "Well, he will have to show me more than what I see. You will always want for things because that young man likes the fast life." Mom, "Can't you see any good in anyone for me? I have dated only two other guys and I'm now twenty-three years old and I love Greg and I'm going to marry him." It seemed that the more Mom showed me that she was displeased with Greg, the closer I cleaved to him. I decided not to have a church wedding. We married in mom's living room. The wedding colors were white and red. It was a beautiful wedding. Everyone seemed happy and they all congratulated us. Three weeks after the wedding, Greg was hired to work with the railroad company. His salary was good, but something happened. He wasn't content with the job. So he quit. He left and went to Los Angeles, California on March 1967. I joined him on June 1, 1967.

On April 24, 1968, Greg and I had our first child, Justin. Greg was working for the naval shipyard and had a very good salary, and he was taking care of his responsibilities. We bought our first car when Justin was only three months old. One particular day, while riding to San Diego, California, I said to Greg, "Let's go home." He said ok. I didn't know really just how homesick I was. I told Greg that California living was too fast for us to rear our child. Living in sunny California was too much. I was used to friendly, caring people, the majority of the time, back home in Richmond, Virginia.

When we arrived home, my mother and sister-in-law were glad to see me. Of course, Mom and Dad and the sisters and brothers were surprised. "Mia, we missed you so much! Are you home to stay?" Oh, no I said, but I knew in my heart that I wanted to stay home only to return to Los Angeles to visit. Greg returned to Los Angeles, California for the remainder of our furniture and things. After returning, he got a job working in a plant and our second child, Donna, was born in 1969. She was delivered at a county hospital where the people who worked there were very inhumane. When I left the hospital, I stayed with

Mom and Dad for a few days to get my strength back and care for my baby. After about six to nine months, Greg left again for California looking for another job. I had finished school where I studied to become a Nurse's Assistant, but I had never worked in that capacity before. I began to look for a job and was later employed at a convalescent home in the dietary department. I loved the patients. After working for about two weeks, Greg was gone now for a month and there wasn't any money except my check of $117.00 every two weeks. I dreaded telling my mother that Greg had not lived up to supporting me and the children while living in her home.

Mom was working the 11-7 shift. She came home the next day a bit angry and began telling me, "You know your husband will not send you and the children any money. You'll be going to California to a nobody. I don't have to like him just because you love him, but he has put all of the responsibility on me. You will pay for the gas to transport your children to the babysitter and for you to be picked up from work. Do you understand?!"

At this time, I was afraid to tell her that I was pregnant with Melody, our third child. I would get up early in the morning and get my children ready. I then walked about one and a half miles to my job to keep from hearing mom fuss about the gas for the car. I worked at my job until I was eight months pregnant, without any problems physically. Emotionally I began to feel rejected and unwanted. I stayed awake one Thursday night, packed my bags and got things somewhat situated with my mother-in-law to keep Justin and Donna until I got a place to live. I left Mom and Dad a note Friday morning telling them that I was gone. Lydia, my younger sister who lived in Texas, let me stay with her for about 2 weeks.

After about seven and a half weeks, there was still no letter or word from Greg. I was infuriated with him. Lydia pleaded with me not to try to find him in Los Angeles. He knew what his responsibilities were already. He can't get away with it, just let it go. He will be the one to lose. By this time, I was hurting and crying, hating the fact that I had to go to substandard living. I fought so hard not to be a welfare recipient. Some of my aunts on my mom's side of the family and also on my dad's stayed with the welfare system. Fortunately, some of them got public jobs later in life.

I didn't want to be like that, their children had less and, in some instances, low self-esteem.

I got somewhat settled and listened to my sister Lydia. It was now Monday and I headed home to Richmond. When I reached my mother-in-law's house, she said, "Both of you act like you are on vacation. My son Greg knows that he has a family in need. He is the children's father." Greg's grandmother was very helpful and protective of him. I guess that was because she had a lot to do with him in his early childhood.

Dr. George saw me the next week, exactly six weeks before Melody was born. He was very rude to me. He was questioning why I didn't stay where I was to have this baby. I answered and said that I didn't have the money, and my husband was out of town without a steady job. As my appointment with the Department of Welfare for emergency help with food stamps and finances approached, by this time, I felt like my world was over. I never knew personally how the welfare system worked.

Greg's grandmother told me to tell them that I didn't know where he was exactly in California, which I really didn't know for a fact. The questions that were asked to qualify for assistance were unreal, but I answered them all. My caseworker was nice to me. When I received my eligibility report, I was granted $89.00 a month in food stamps and $113.00 a month for AFDC, very little for a mother and three children. Most nights I would stay awake because I was pregnant with only four weeks before Melody was to be born. I slept with Greg's grandmother and my two small children, my feet hanging off the bed most of the time. My sister Geraldine was renting from an elderly lady who had a considerably large house. She told me to come and live with her. I was so relieved. She made sure that I ate properly and got the rest that was long overdue for me. I prayed and asked God not to let me have to live with Mom and Dad for a while. I didn't think that I could handle mom's ridicule and having to go through the emotional trauma I was experiencing because I was let down by a husband who I thought loved me and cared for me and his children. I had to face the situation or perish. I could have easily blamed others and made excuses, but it wouldn't have helped. I had to make a quality decision. I am determined to rear three small children and take care of myself. No time to cry over spilled milk, my Auntie Zelma would say. I now understood why she said this. I was only a child at that time.

On September 25, 1970, Melody was born. My sister Ada and her husband helped me to get to a private hospital in our hometown. Melody weighed 9 pounds. After 2 days we were able to go home. As time went on, the house got a bit crowded at Ada's. I made calls in the area for housing and prepared to move to my own place again. Melody was now four months old, and I thought I had better start to get a profession, knowing I had fallen away from my dreams and aspiration to be a speech and drama teacher as well as a professional singer. I had all the respect and admiration for nurses. So I called the vocational schools to see what it took and how to begin studying for a career to support me and my children.

Somehow, Mrs. Evelyn Bias, a professional businesswoman, must have heard about me wanting to do something with my life. Oh, my prayer to God was answered; for Him not to let me ever be totally dependent on any family member to take care of me. The face washings I got from the family every time they saw me were awful concerning Greg's negligence towards us. I swallowed it and in spite of it all, it caused me to become more determined than ever to accomplish my goals. I knew I had the ability and potential to be somebody responsible and productive in society.

June 1971, Mrs. Evelyn Bias told me to go to the vocational school or call to see what they had to offer. They mentioned accounting, typing and all types of clerical studies, but since I liked nursing, it was my choice. My short-term course as a certified nurse's assistant helped me in my selection of study. I started to study all of the prerequisites to enter the nursing class to become a vocational nurse. Still dealing with the shame of being on welfare, I couldn't understand why it seemed to linger with me, but it didn't change my mind. I was more determined to accomplish my goal: to live a comfortable, fruitful life. I could hear Mom's voice saying, as she always did, "You have to face reality; your daddy and I didn't rear any of you with welfare assistance," with just this in my imagination it kept me fighting to come up from the bottom. The stigma of welfare was not a good feeling. I felt it was always for the elderly and disabled people, not the young who could turn things around by using it only to step up. I saw too many young mothers and single women with children who had made it (welfare) a way of life, pursuit and happiness, really a crutch, not a stepping stone. This was a panic situation; all I was thinking about at this time was my children and the fact that I was trapped and what if I didn't get help from the public welfare system. I never let go of my hope of being a nurse, while my children were ages three, four, and thirteen months. Knowing I couldn't entertain the idea that Greg had turned his back on us, some of the older women of the church would encourage me. They would say to me, "Mia, you can make it; men, only some men walk away from their families. Just don't give up." I called Mrs. Evelyn Bias again and she told me to go to the vocational school and tell them that I wanted to be a Vocational Nurse. I did this with prayer in my heart, Lord, just let me get into the vocation of nursing and I will give my job back to you. Lord, I will do my job as unto you and I know it will be ok. In September I received a call from the school to meet with the counselor who worked with financially handicapped mothers who received AFDC. I began to get more eager with anticipation to get things on the up rise for me and my children. Through my appointment with Mrs. Hayes, I was informed that the state would pay for my schooling and maintenance, the daycare and provide daycare at home for Melody, who was fifteen months. Daycare wasn't accepting children her age. I was so thrilled to hear such news because I thought that my kids and I were doomed and destined for poverty with only $113.00 a month to live on. In September of 1970, I started pre-study courses to enter school for the following January. Everything was set. The state made all payments to daycare for the children. All of my school books and supplies were taken care of as well. Mom seemed to have been more understanding. She would help me with the children while I attended pre-nursing classes getting ready for my career. To my surprise, there was many other welfare recipients' taking advantage of what the Department of Public Welfare was doing to help people who had qualified financially for the program.

It had been five months now. My friends and I went to the nursing service personnel and stated that we were interested in employment. Sister Mary St. John was eager to hire us for afternoons, after classes. We filled out the applications and were called to work the following week. Sister St. John told us we could have a floor preference to work. The 3-11 shift Supervisor may have to ask us to work on other floors. After being on the job for almost a month, I had to report my financial income to my caseworker at the Department of Welfare. When my next eligibility report came for further public assistance, it was reduced to $9.00 a month because I was bringing home a monthly check of $178.00. My wages for working on a public job was more than the AFDC check that I received monthly. They allowed me to keep the $89.00 food stamps each month. Even though this job only paid me $56.00 more than my AFDC check before they reduced it, working out on my own as a nurse's assistant until I graduated from Richmond Vocational School was much easier to work with. I gained a more secure and positive out-look on providing for my family as a single parent.

It was now time for me to start making plans for getting my licenses to practice as a Vocational Nurse. Fourteen months of studying, ups and downs, but I saw myself accomplishing my goals with a Nursing Career. It finally happened in March of 1973. Just two months before graduation, my nursing class had a banquet. Greg had just returned home.

This was his first-time seeing Melody. He was very apologetic for not living up to the standards of a man and father who had a family. He said, "Mia, will you forgive me? I didn't fair in Los Angeles like you thought, I did." "Greg, after not hearing from you, I resented your being so unconcerned about us. I won't have to depend on the welfare to help me any longer because in two months I will be graduating from Richmond Vocational School, and I will get me a full-time job. I have been managing without you quite well. I was thinking that my situation was so bad, but it turned out that you made it possible for me to be on welfare thereby being a good thing after all, I am stepping up. I've taken advantage of what it had to offer. Thank you so much my darling husband. I could have easily stayed in a pitiful party, folding my hands, crying and wondering where and when you would face being a parent. My facing this letdown in my life helped me to deal with it realistically. I had a problem and it had to be solved. I was in it to come out of it. As mom always said, 'No matter what life brings your way, you must face reality'. My attitude changed.

It was the reason that my outcome about being put on welfare proved to be my stepping stone and not a crutch. My graduation is in a few weeks. I am going to apply for a 90-day graduate position. My licenses should be back after then. A licensed Vocational Nurse is what I will be. I can then work any place I choose because I paid the price to labor and get something."

After this conversation, Greg became very repentant and asked me to forgive him and give him another chance to be the husband and father that I wanted him to be. Since this had been my desire all along, I decided to give him that opportunity to prove himself. We resolved to come back together as a family, rear our children, and eventually purchase a house for them.

I graduated and afterward applied for my nursing permit. The intensity of waiting for my nursing permit was almost unbearable but when the day arrived, I was ecstatic. I immediately called Mrs. Neilson, the Director of Nursing Service at Olen Health Care and placed my application for employment. Two weeks passed and I telephoned Mrs. Neilson, who informed me of a nursing shortage and that she needed me to fill in at the nursing home on the 3-11 Shift. I was very glad to accept the offer since I lived near the nursing home! I could drop my children off at the babysitter on the way to work. This worked out just fine. After 90 days of working, my nursing license came, and I was then a licensed Vocational Nurse.

About a year later, we moved to Greenland Housing Authority, which better accommodated my growing family.

I worked for several years, but Greg seemed to still maintain his old pattern of not being able to hold down a steady job. His social life—partying, nightclubs, marijuana smoking, extramarital relationships, and unsavory friends—remained the same as it had always been. His lifestyle took him away from home a great deal of the time, along with the money needed to take care of the family. Even though I was married to him, I could not depend on him to support his family.

After four years of working at Olen Health Care, I became pregnant with our fourth child. Greg, true to form, left me to walk this road alone again as he had done before. But after a short period of time, Greg, who had moved back to California, began to send money back to us. Our child Kevin was born in August and Greg came back to live with us in the end of September and began work shortly thereafter. Within a two-year period, I applied for work at a county hospital and was hired to work with pediatric and female medicine patients. I later worked with the Psych and Detox unit. We purchased our own home shortly thereafter and Greg tried to be a better husband and father. But the constant pressure of dealing with deep-seated insecurities caused him to go even deeper into his immoral lifestyle.

My heart's desire had always been to have a loving, Christian family because I grew up in one myself. But because I was young and immature and left alone so much with the responsibility of the household, being mom and dad, I began to experiment with nightclubs and partying. But I quickly realized it did not satisfy me. I was more concerned with the proper training and welfare of my little children as opposed to me having a "good time". I realized that if I wanted my children not to go astray, I had to be willing to make the sacrifice to build a solid and strong foundation for them to grow. As I attended school and church, standards for living a different lifestyle was important because I was the greater influence in the lives of my children—a role model.

From Welfare To Prosperity

As time went on, I began to make discoveries of more potential that God had placed on the inside of me, being fruitful and multiplying not just to bring children into the world but to prosper His people by utilizing my talents, gifts, potential, and abilities, thereby duplicating productive living and good character. My struggle to live above what the welfare system had to offer became a dream come true. I was committed to doing a task to rise above almost indigent poverty type living. Through this I went from welfare to prosperity. I pursued with persistence and attained and accomplished my goals. I knew that if I could do it, many other welfare recipients would be able to do it also. They have to look at it as a no-living situation, but since they are a part of it, make it their stepping stone. This is only if those who want to rise up and stop the vicious cycle of welfare and having it as a crutch, which is a generational curse, begin to see them using it temporarily, not as a complete way of life. There are too many young women in the United States of America who are complacent, lazy and think that all they have to do is go to the mailbox and get a check. I didn't want this as a lifestyle for my children. I birthed my children into the world, and I was responsible for taking care of them. I wanted my freedom because the Department of Welfare has rules and guidelines that seem enslaving and making a cripple of women. This was saying to me that you cannot live a better life, in my opinion. I kept telling myself that I could do better than just take the crumbs from the table of the Department of Welfare and wear the stigma of

<u>there goes another one of them, the welfare thieves and robbers of the taxpayers' hard-earned money.</u> Never really fully satisfied being on welfare, I sought to improve and upgrade myself; had a public job before the crisis came into my life of a man, I married at the age of twenty-three. He was the same age, but he was not yet mature enough to commit to taking on a man's role. Mom always taught me and my five sisters that your child will not carry your maiden name. You must be married and the man that fathers your children, you will have his name. I will not have any illegitimate grandchildren. I respected this in my mom. Mom was just straight forward with the facts of life. Her teachings early in life proved to help me become who I am today. Achieving success and desires successfully ends by staying on course, never giving up when times got hard or more severe. I knew victories would be my reward and testimony to many I was around daily.

This book is shared with single women across the United States of America, who are welfare recipients or those who are thinking about using the welfare system. Use it as a step up from where you are not as a crutch and crippling factor. It offers women more in a way of prevention as opposed to the past, letting you now get an education, finish high school, acquire advanced degrees in any field of desired education. The welfare system is not the end result for your life, only if you as women and mothers allow it to be. Rise up! Who wants to stop the repeated cycle? Just because your grandmother and your mother used the system as a crutch, doesn't mean that you have to. This may be the only way of life that you know, but you can make it your stepping stone so that your daughters and sons can have a better life. It's hard but it's fair, life off welfare is good. You are in control of what's happening in your life. There are millions of single women who have to take on the total family responsibility of the home. We don't need to create problems by duplicating welfare crutches. The small amount of money that you get for an extra child born into this world is not worth your taking the time to get pregnant and add extra burdens of five to six children of fathers who just walk away and act like they have no responsibilities to that child or children.

I exhort and encourage you to make a decision to go from welfare to prosperity and make welfare your stepping stone. Believe in yourself! You have something positive in you, the creator of good things. Don't be discouraged and linger in self-pity. Men are still telling women lies about what they are going to do to help you and your children, and it never gets done. I had to turn a deaf ear to my condition and begin to see myself with a vision and a goal to accomplish. Men, not facing up to their responsibilities of being the breadwinners for their families and having to be taken to court for child support, are not the men to spend their valuable time with. By the time procedures are finished, you are tired, torn and worn from filling out the papers to get the wages deducted from his pay on the job.

Make a decision about your relationships. Does he want to be responsible? Will he be a good father for your children, or will he be a drifter with a meaningless life? Does he know or have a purpose in life? If not, it's an aimless lifestyle without character, morals, and Christian values. When these things are absent, we are destined to perish because we are without the plan and purpose of God in our lives to sustain our livelihood with a balance. When you purpose it in your heart, as a single woman on welfare with one or more children, don't allow your life to stop there. Know that you can do better for yourself. Making a step toward future enrichment and using the system in a positive way can improve things and make good things happen. You must know you have on the inside of you God's creative ability because it was predestined from the beginning of creation that you and I have gifts, talents, abilities and potential to be that unique person cultivating good things. God put these things on the inside of every human being on this earth for the benefits of one's self and others.

Your life doesn't have to stop there in the welfare system because it only creates a duplication of more generational welfare curses. You want more out of life than to see your daughter and granddaughter on welfare all of their lives. You want them to pursue other avenues to become educated and successful and gainfully employed, basically an asset to society and wherever their world takes them. You want them to be women in society, living and giving back to the community. Stopping at the welfare status is saying to yourself, "I cannot do better, go no further and my children's lives and mine stops here." This to me is one of the most negative attitudes one can have because of the impact it will have on the lives of your children as well as yourself. Your situation can turn around, for it all lies in the decisions you make now in your present situation. You cannot allow yourself to become comfortable. Use everything offered to you by the Public Welfare system. Educate yourself if you have not completed high school and get your GED. Advance to a Vo-Tech school or college because you are better equipping yourself for the future. Advanced knowledge means higher paying jobs and salaries. Welfare can be a way out of being the limited person that society has put down. You have to develop the attitude of refusing to stay on the bottom, barely getting alone. Sometimes it means you have to give up relationships by taking a positive look and evaluating this person. Is this person one who is enhancing me and my children? If someone in your life is already down, it is like the blind leading the blind which means both will fall in the ditch. No one is going anywhere because there is seemingly no hope and everyone perishes. They have no aspirations, dreams, visions or goals to work toward.

You need to have goals and accomplish them. Have a vision; see yourself being above only and not beneath.

How do we see ourselves? We are who we think in a positive or negative way. When we imagine things, it forms IMAGES. For example, when we imagine a flower, our mind begins to see the image of a flower. Notice it's the same way we think about ourselves.

Proverbs 23:7

As a man thinketh in his heart, so is he.

If my thoughts are of exalting, my actions will be those gravitating toward and getting involved in the thing that would cause me to come from where I am, acquainting myself with others going in the direction of positive things, improving my situation by incorporating Biblical principles to my life, as we launch forward to improve. We are born for a purpose. I cannot emphasize enough. According to Jeremiah 1:5, "Before I formed you in the womb, I knew thee and before thou came forth out of the womb. I sanctified thee, and I ordained thee a prophet to the nations." God is speaking today to us His people. Whoever He made us to be and to do in this earth was already predestined from the foundation of the world. There is something on the inside of us God has put there for us to live a bountiful life. We are His workmanship created in Christ Jesus for good works which God prepared beforehand that we should walk in them.

II Corinthians 5:17 Therefore, if any man is in Christ, he is a new creature: old things are passed away; behold, all things become new.

From this point our associations are different. We do things that are pleasing before God and man, not looking or turning again to our old ways of the past. Fellowshipping with other Christians, attending a church where the gospel is preached and taught in the local assembly, wherein you become spiritually strengthened! Things appear very different and they are. You have something to offer and share with others, not only in the church setting but everywhere your world takes you. Making better choices and decisions influences our lives greatly.

We must constantly download our MINDS with the Word of God as we take the time to read it, meditate on it, live it by faith, mixing the Word of God with our faith, speaking it out of our mouth, receiving and believing that the Word of God is the Absolute TRUTH concerning us.

The manifestation of what we say and think in our minds and hearts must agree and it will come to pass. I am going to buy a car and a house, making preparations to bring this to pass.

You said that it stops. No longer will I subject my life and the lives of my children to this. I now have a better and more prosperous life, one that will qualify me to earn a good living and give me the ability to have the comforts and necessities needed in my life.

You are equipped to give back into the lives of your children and others around you with the assurance of knowing you have positive in you, and you can have the positive attitude that you can make things better. No more bearing the label of being lazy and waiting for someone to take care of you. You are God's creation. He made you a unique individual with a plan and a purpose for your life. On the inside of you are treasures. I challenge you to start your search for who you are in Christ. Our success in life lies in Christ; we are complete in Him.

My Identity, How I See Myself Today

I am who I am today because first of all who God intended me to be. I know my purpose in life and I am fulfilling it. I am preparing now to pursue the ministry, a greater measure for the sake of humanity and the many suffering and lost souls. Sharing my life story will cause many to see hope. I have great satisfaction in my life being a health care provider and spreading God's Word. My monthly income went from $113.00 a month to $1600.00 a month. These things happened because of the Almighty GOD and the opportunities I utilized. I saw welfare as my opportunity to increase in knowledge, better job security, a way to provide the medical experience for my children and myself, get other things that were necessary for family living in way of shelter and maintenance vehicles. I was very determined to change the image others had of me while being on welfare.

Instead of taking from myself and my children, I added. My children didn't know anything until later. I made mention of it to them as pre-teens and the truth they accepted from me. Looking back over the years, I am so grateful for not giving up. I am seeing today my persistence and consistent pattern of achieving success paid off. My fortitude to stand and never give up, I attribute to God and a good mother, a very strong person in the home as I was growing up. Her positions about life helped me. I now see myself equipped for the future. I can be employed wherever I choose working in a nursing capacity. As a nurse, I have spent nineteen and a half years working for the state, accepting advice from positive people, people who told me that I could make it in life, and I would be the one to change my course or remain in the fallen state of being on welfare. It is only so far that you could go using the AFDC check that only increases by having another child. Today, I have no regrets about welfare because It Became My Stepping Stone to a better way of living. The same thing can happen to you. Challenges, obstacles and circumstances that come to you, take a stand and don't take your eyes off your dreams or visions. A person without a vision perishes. Proverbs 29:18 Where there is no vision, the people PERISH.

What Is Welfare/Afdc

"What is the purpose of AFDC?" It has been allocated to provide food and clothing to needy families. Public Assistance is widely used by individuals with dependent children, based on the need. AFDC is granted to homes with no father in the home. AFDC is sometimes granted with fathers in the home under certain circumstances. AFDC can be seen as a relief from the burden of being financially deprived. There is much criticism of Welfare today. Many in society believe that any able-bodied people can work for an honest living. This would provide financial assistance for the elderly, handicapped, and disabled. It has been stated that today's young woman continues to have children only to increase her check. In many areas, for years states have proven that there are more single mothers between the ages of fifteen and nineteen with three or more children on welfare. Some states are being judged very harshly for trying to get mothers to be more productive with their lives.

The welfare system did not change the inside of you. You made a change in your life because God placed something good in all of us. Some of us chose to use it and others do not, no matter what price is paid to live in poverty. Complacency is a dead-end decision

Breaking The Generational Curse Of Welfare

<u>Realize</u> that you are operating under a curse (which is harmful because of its crippling effects). It can only be broken through the power of God. Make a decision the cycle stops at me; no more being hindered, cannot make it. Know that you are created for a purpose and there is a divine plan for your life, established in this earth for you by God. <u>Be determined</u> that you will rise up and be all that you can be for the glory of God. Sometimes it means getting out of relationships of other females. Some of their thinking is I am born for failure, going no place, doing nothing, getting no place at all. This means that the relationship with this man and that man has to end. Most times he is drifting from other females' homes, creating more lives to suffer (innocent children) not taking care of anyone of them and keeping you reapplying for welfare and food stamps. You were born in the world for much more than this. As a woman decides not to be a baby factory, when the Scripture said be fruitful and multiply. Genesis 1:22 KJV, and God blessed them saying, be fruitful and multiply. This means whatever talent, gift, and ability Creator God placed on the inside of you is to be developed, for the purpose of you being the reaper of good things, prosperity, health, wealth, successful life, careers, obedient, respectable, educated children, Christian and moral living, not to be shaped and fashioned by the welfare (government) system. Doing things God's ways always have the better outcome.

Begin to associate with people going places and being successful in life. Since every man is created equal but yet unique and individually the way He wanted us to be, begin to seek Him to find out what it is that He wants you to do, how to come to know Him, as Lord, making Him the King of your heart. It's a challenge to become who you are from what the devil has led you to believe about yourself. Come to know Jesus. He will accept you back, when the friends and the parties turn their backs on you. If you believe in your heart and confess with your mouth the Lord Jesus, your life is changed from doing things your way. Now it's done God's way: Romans 10:9, 10 KJV "That if thou shalt confess with thy mouth the Lord Jesus, and shalt believe in thine heart that God hath raised him from the dead, thou shalt be saved. Verse 10, For with the heart man believeth unto righteousness; and with the mouth confession is made unto salvation." If any man be in Christ, walking in the newness of life causes you and inspires you to be who you are changed from within, II Cor. 5:17. Continue to separate yourself from people who have made the choice to stay in their condition of regression. The Word declares in II Cor. 6: 17, 18 wherefore come out from among them and be ye separate says the Lord, and touch not the unclean thing and I will receive you. And will be a Father unto you, and ye shall be my sons and daughters says the Lord Almighty. Continue to let the light of God shine through you, lifting up Jesus with your life style changed. It will cause the people you used to be around to desire and hunger for what you have, your new life in Christ, blessing and possessing everywhere you go. It costs you something to live holy before God. Stay before Him because the work He started in you, He is faithful to complete it. Allow God to keep you in His perfect ways. You will live with His promise for you and your children, not beneath the promises of God. II Cor. 7:1, "Having therefore these promises, dearly beloved, let us cleanse ourselves from all filthiness of the flesh and spirit, perfecting holiness in the fear of God."

You are an example in your home and community impacting and influencing the lives of others in a positive or negative way. In the home, you have to be mother and father for your little children, double roles to play. As a female, there are little girls who need to know the right way to live and conduct themselves as ladies. Her success in life as well as other siblings depends on the picture you are painting as woman, mother, head of your house and everything else. Take no thought—brooding over the guys who were not committed to you for each one of your pregnancies, discovering that he has children in at least 2 or more homes. Begin to deal with it in a positive attitude: I am on this road and I have to travel it, make it for me and my children to be successful in life. The way to enhance and continue to move forward is to be persistent and consistent in the things that you do that make life better for you and your children. Before you were born, God already knew you and who and what would transpire in your life, whether caused by your own efforts or the doings of others to bring about a positive or negative change in your life. How you respond to change in your life determines your outcome.

God empowers us to do all things through Him according to Philippians 4:13. All of our needs as single women with many little children are met through Christ Jesus according to Philippians 4:19. Riches for us are untold in the glory of God. Getting in His glory is fulfilling every need through prayer and reading and meditating His Word and keeping it before us, according to Joshua 1:8. Jesus is the One who causes us to have wealth according to Deut. 8:18 and Deut. 7: 8, 9. Begin to cultivate the things God has placed on the inside, your abilities, gifts, and talents. It is His desire to see you prosper in good works, in good health, even as your soul prospers. Allow God to shape and mold you the way He wants to. Since you have now made the decision that the generational curse of welfare stops at you, the broken cycle of it, then your daughters and sons will see life differently instead of defeat and being deprived, just simply without, not being able to have self-sufficient, noble character, Christian living, achieving success in school and pursuing careers motivated by your change and outlook on life. The greater One lives on the inside of you. He is greater than he that is in the world. He's constantly moving on the inside bringing that great change in your life and your children's lives ending the curse of welfare from generation to generation of your children and your children's children. Ask God for forgiveness of mothers who were blind with no vision which caused much inflicted suffering to their children. You ask for forgiveness because of you partaking. Also, confess to God, as He sees and knows the intent and motive in the hearts of man, according to Luke 23:34 and Proverbs 28:3. Ask Jesus to cleanse you after He has forgiven you. His blood never loses the power to cleanse us from all righteousness according to I John 1:7-9. According to Philippians 2: 12-13 submit your will to God, allowing it to become God's will, James 4:7. As you strive to do it God's way, your lifestyle in Christ will greatly influence the spiritual growth of your children, family, friends and relations. Feeding on the Word of God will do wonders. Read 1 Peter 2:2 and John 7: 37, 38.

Set goals, and become a person of vision, never taking your eyes off your aspirations. Continue to focus on this fact that God created you for a purpose. Fulfill it, always seeking Him for directions. Of all people created, He made you special and uniquely different from anyone else in the world, in the image and likeness of Himself He created you. There is no one who can do better in what God created you for than you. In the beginning, He loved you. He put on the inside of you the ability to do and achieve also. God is just, Righteous and Holy. He gave all of mankind ability to creatively do various things so that He would be glorified. Realize what He has placed in your hands. There is much to offer. He gives to mankind witty inventions according to Proverbs 8:12. Allow the scope of your vision to be big. It's ok to think big. Our Father God is a big God and it's His desire to bless His people. Stay in the race, be steadfast, immovable and always abounding in the truth of the Word of God. This race is not given to the swift or strong, but to the one that endures to the end. Surely victory and success is the expected end.

When Christ went to the cross, He took care of all the things that would hinder us and keep us from living and receiving the blessed promises, I Peter 3:9. The faithfulness of our Father God to His people, promises, Word and His covenant, He never takes away because of our ways. He spoke it in His Word, it shall come to pass. His word concerning us is forever settled in heaven. We must continue to stand on the Word of God, even though there are many dictates, obstacles, situations and circumstances. The adversary, the devil, brings them to uproot what you have planted, your goals being to live a righteous, holy life, your commitment to Christ, developing and cultivating your talents and gifts for the kingdom of God. He does all of this to make you go back to (Egypt) bondage of welfare but you must stand because you made a decision that the cycle of the generational curse of welfare stopped at you and that you now know who you are, the purpose for your life and the will of God also. Take your stand of faith: choose to walk by faith no matter what the dictates are around you in day-to-day living, not moved by what you see, for we walk by faith not by sight, II Cor. 5:7.

According to II Chronicles 20:15, the walls of opposition must leave when God's got it because He cares so much for us. He watches over us with a jealous love. Cast every care upon Him. He bares all burdens and moves misery and strife. He is the greatest burden bearer. II Cor. 12: 9, 10 says, "And He said unto me, My grace is sufficient for thee: for my strength is made perfect in weakness. Most gladly therefore will I rather glory in my infirmities, that the power of Christ may rest upon me. Therefore I take pleasure in infirmities, in reproaches, in necessities, in persecutions, in distresses for Christ's sake: for when I am weak, then am I strong."

Keep your dreams and visions before you. Don't let anyone sway you. Too long this plague has swallowed up, destroyed, decayed millions of families for decades with no hope, no aspirations to go beyond the welfare cycle. This is the way the government system operates. It offers some things but what's on the inside of you is greater because your will and ability is the bottom line. God created you not the welfare system. It's limited but God is not! A challenge to change—become a person of vision, seeing it, talking it, walking in it according to Proverbs 29:18, without a vision, the people perish. See yourself above, not beneath. You can do it.

My Vision For Women

My vision for women is for them to see themselves as women of destiny and vision by coming to the realization of who they really are perceiving that they were created for more than just to give birth to children in this world but that they can be fruitful and multiply in other areas of life as well. Because of the gifts, talents and abilities that God has placed on the inside of each woman, they can choose to break the generational curse of welfare by using every available resource in order to improve themselves. Millions of young women are heads of households and the challenge to change their circumstances is great. But there's hope! Learning the Word of God which reveals His will for humanity, these women can rise up and change their lives spiritually, emotionally, academically, financially and economically. My vision is that women will stand up and dare to be different by deciding and choosing God's way and to realize that they are unique, original and special in God's sight… the apple of God's eye, Deuteronomy 32:10.

Personal Expression

Being a woman who has experienced being a single parent, seemingly caught up in the vicious cycle of the welfare system, I understand, first hand, the feelings of rejection and low self-esteem. God has healed me, delivered me and set me free by His mighty power. And He has raised me up to bring that same freedom to women whose minds are enslaved by thinking that their circumstances and the conditions of their lives cannot change. Today, because of God's Word, I know who I am in Christ Jesus and that He has called, anointed and appointed me to tell women everywhere that there is hope. My burning desire is to let women know that they were created for much more than what they are settling for. If nothing changes, then nothing changes. Where you are at this very moment as you read this book is not where you are going to be. In order to keep the same condition is to do nothing. For certain you will definitely have the same results. In simple words, to get something different, you have to do something different. Women are one of the most valuable creatures God has put on earth.

I Will Rise From Where I Am

I will stop the wrestle, for I am a vessel, with
unlimited treasures that cannot be measured,
by man. I have risen from
where I am, stuck in a jam,
no thank you ma'am. Fame is
what I see, not just a glee I am free,
you see, that's me.
I have risen from where I am.
Calm, courageous, consistent, and persistent,
I will sail and not fail at nothing I do.
Now I know who I am, Where I am
going and my purpose here
on this great planet Earth. I
never dreamed or envisioned how
really good life could be,
Only to find out after rising from where I am.
The deepest treasure on the inside of me,
Oh some hadn't been tapped into, you see.
What awesome things I've come to know.
Creation keeps springing up out of my inner being
It's a wonder to see me!

Going places, doing things, touching the lives of others
all because I decided to rise up from where I am.

God did His part when He created me, No one

else can do what He created me for. Know

that I am the Lord's and He's working in me

and through me,

Is marvelous in His sight, because He is the One who

causes me to rise from where I am.

Our minds renewed, change our actions when we begin to renew our minds to a better way of thinking. Things around us take on another change in appearance. There is power in Dr. Norman Vincent Peale's book. During my teenage years, my mother would read it and have us read the same book. I didn't realize its worth until I was in my adult years.

Romans 12: 1-2 I beseech you therefore brethren, by the mercies of God, that ye present your bodies a living sacrifice, holy, acceptable unto God, which is your reasonable services.

Verse 2 And be not conformed to this world: but be ye transformed by the renewing of your mind, that ye may prove what is that good, and acceptable, and perfect, will of God.

Matthew 6:33 But seek ye first the kingdom of God, and His righteousness; and all these things shall be added unto you.

God must be our first priority in all that we do. This makes other things much more pleasant and the flow much easier. Begin to say daily what God says about you in His Holy Word—you read from the Bible. I am made in the image and likeness of God.

Genesis 1:26, 27 And God said, let us make man in our image, after our likeness: and let them have dominion over the fish of the sea, and over the fowl of the air, and over the cattle, and over all the earth, and over every creeping thing that creepeth upon the earth.

Verse 27 So God created man in His own image, in the image of God created He him; male and female created He them.

We chart the course of our lives by what we speak and do. Words are seeds that contain our future and this present time we live in. We must be very careful about words spoken over us.

Proverbs 18:21 Death and life are in the power of the tongue: and they that love it shall eat the fruit thereof.

Matthew 12:37 For by thy words thou shalt be justified, and by thy words thou shalt be condemned.

There is a reaping of words we have carelessly spoken, thought and done which have caused us to experience some struggles and hardships in our lives. It takes rehearsing and practicing the Word of God to build and edify with positive spoken words, based on a spiritual principal.

Matthew 15:18 But those things which proceed out of the mouth come forth from the heart; and they defile the man.

See yourself from the heart with a higher standard living above the system of welfare. See yourself rising from fast food employment to owning a restaurant. If you are interested in cooking, there are schools for culinary art. Also, there's clothing, being a designer, the CEO of your company with you as owner. Remain focused. You have a dream, an idea. See it as complete and you will give much definition of who you are, unique, fearfully and wonderfully made by God. People can imitate you, but they cannot duplicate you. You are the only one of your kind. God didn't make a mistake when He created you. God wants you to fulfill His purpose and assignment in His earth. Do it well. You will feel great with a sense of accomplishment. God's creative ability is flowing out of you all because you made the right decision, got involved in productivity, completing your chosen profession, devoting your time and effort to live in a corporate world with the best paying jobs, encouraging others to likewise. After you have been strengthened, continue to give encouragement to others.

This change comes through Holy Spirit whereby we become strengthen and renewed by putting on the newness of life, spoken of earlier, a new creation in Christ, the old ways of the flesh are done away with no longer doing things as the world dictates.

Psalm 51:10 Create in me a clean heart O God; and renew a right spirit within me.

Ephesians 4:23-24 And be renewed in the spirit of your mind;

Verse 24 And that ye put on the new man, which after God is created in righteousness and true holiness.

This new man is the born-again spirit on the inside of us and cannot sin.

Principal Keys For Daily Living

. Don't forget your smile today because it adds to your face value.

. Laughter does good as medicine. It's an important part of your daily living.

. Your ability to take control of your situation determines your success in life.

. It's never too late to improve yourself. Start building a network of self-improvement in the lives of others around you.

. Don't be fooled about what others say about you, what you don't know about yourself compliments you.

Proverbs 23:7 For as a man thinks in his heart so is he.

. Honesty is the best policy; integrity pays well.

. Turn opposition into a challenge from which you can learn from. It will lead you to SUCCESS.

. Never underestimate your ability to IMPROVE your situation. In all reality, you can. HOW BAD DO YOU WANT IT?

. Make up your mind to be successful. It's not based on where you are now. It's where you want to go in life. LIVE OUT YOUR DREAMS.

. A fall today doesn't mean you will fail tomorrow. Stay focused; shake yourself; get back up. You are the only star that can play the role and play it well.

. Grow stronger in RESISTING the TEMPTATION to anything that has held you down and held you back from climbing the awesome ladder of success.

. Take the limits off. You are the one holding yourself back, just as a fruit jar cannot open and the fruit cannot be poured out without your removing the lid. The contents cannot come out of the jar unless you open the jar. It's the same way when you keep inside your talents. You are in charge of your condition or situation. Be determined for change and to end all dead relations whether with a male or female. If the children's father is in and out of your lives, what's in it for you and your children? When a man is a drifter, he has nothing to bring to the table or to offer you. He doesn't have or hold a steady job. He lies and comes with alibis and many broken promises. Admit there is absolutely nothing in it for you.

. Whatever living arrangements, someone who wants to shack up with you and live with you for what you can provide, when the only person who is supposed to benefit from your AFDC is you and your children. Wake up and see the bigger picture facing the reality of it. It's a deeper shanking into the perils of poverty living. Living substandard is beneath the privileges of what God has planned for your life according to Jeremiah.

Jeremiah 29:11 For I know the thoughts that I think toward you, saith the Lord, thoughts of peace and not evil, to give you an expected end.

The way things are in your present state isn't what God has for you because the endless cycle of welfare continues as you make no effort to think or desire better or to end welfare, wherein your children could have learned how they see mom as the positive role model in the home who greatly influence the outcome of her children's lives. Yes, it's a sacrifice to give up what makes you feel good because he may have told you he loved you. With all the negative actions, you don't know where he is most times. He never has any money; makes excuses about finding employment. He cannot buy needed things for the baby such as pampers, formula, and clothing. He cannot show up at PTO meetings or parent/teacher conferences concerning your children. Get real. This man is at the zero level but if you evaluate it and really look at it, only God can take you to a real hero who will really love, appreciate, and respect you for being the real woman. Every relationship is different. Some men are responsible and want to marry you and be the provider and take care of the responsibility of the home (family). He spends time with the children nurturing them and teaching his sons how to not just be men but be responsible and caring men by exhibiting this lifestyle in the home so that the children can follow the trend of their father and mother. Children learn from whatever environment they are in. It is a wonderful thing to change as a single woman. Every decision made, good or bad, influences her home. In order to see positive change, positive decisions must be made. No matter what outer influences are present because there are consequences to every decision we make in life.

God has given us everything to live out the abundant life in this earth. He is not pleased when we make choices that cause lack and suffering in our lives. He suffered all things for those of us who dare to believe in Him, invite Him to live in us and through us for His Glory.

John 10:10 The abundant Life.

The thief (devil) cometh not, but for to steal, and to kill and to destroy: I am come that they might have life, and that they might have it more abundantly.

God's plan has always been one for us to prosper and be in good health even as our souls prosper, healthy and wealthy. This can be done by getting to school, preparing and developing skills that will qualify us for good jobs with better pay. All that's on the inside just needs developing and training for the benefit of you and your household. Resist fear because it paralyzes your faith which can hinder faith from operating in your life. Fear erases your 'I can do it'. Stop listening to negative voices speaking negative words. Quickly make your exit from girlfriends or anyone who is speaking such as, "Girl, if I were you, I wouldn't be getting up early in the morning riding the bus to school and missing all of my Soap Operas, having to study on the weekends, staying up late at night with books, writing reports and getting someone to keep my children while I catch a ride to the public library." Think about it, you are going places (positive) in life and accomplishing your goals to improve your living condition. Your children's father or fathers haven't gotten qualified yet by upgrading themselves. It's all up to you to choose to get off Welfare or to stay. If your girlfriend was you, she would be doing exactly what you are doing. After obtaining, you will be approached with many negative statements. Some demeaning, humiliating and laughter by others but you cannot allow this to stop you.

Keep turning a deaf ear. It is with the sacrifice you are making to have a different lifestyle off welfare. I can assure you of my personal experiences as a welfare recipient. It paid off for me to stay focused and surround myself with positive people. I wanted my children to be developed spiritually, emotionally, socially, psychologically and to know that they could be productive in life and to give back into the lives of others as they grew up from childhood to adults themselves.

Peter 1: 2-3 Grace and peace be multiplied unto you through the knowledge of God, and of Jesus our Lord.

According as His divine power hath given unto us all things that pertain unto life and godliness through the knowledge of Him that hath called us to glory and virtue.

What If I Had Stayed Connected To The Welfare System

As you have read in the previous chapter, I was on welfare with my three older children. Had I remained with the system, would my oldest daughter have become a person in the professional world as a Register Nurse (RN), married 14 years, studying and advancing in the field of nursing as a Nurse Practitioner in medical and surgical care? She is a born-again Christian who is serious about her spiritual life; enjoys teaching and working with children. Melody, my youngest daughter, works as a dietary aid in childcare. She hasn't decided to start her Daycare Facility for small children at this time, but it is her desire to have a business of this kind.

My oldest son, Justin, has a diversity of interests and different jobs. Now he engages in rearing horses to involve them in racing one day.

The youngest of my children, Kevin, was very inquisitive and would explore as a toddler. I had more time to spend with him. I noticed his interest in the medical profession when he was only 2 years of age. He told me that he was a doctor. The impact of this coming from a child his age was so profound that I started calling him who he was, a doctor of course with his toy doctor's medical bag, in his childish way at the county Hospital. When Kevin was 4 years of age, he was struck by an automobile, injuring his right thigh resulting in a midshaft fracture, (greenstick) placed in traction for months in the hospital. There, he changed his profession to being an Orthopedic Surgeon. Kevin said, "Mom I am going to fix people broken bones so they can walk again like me." God blessed my child to not have any defects in his gait while walking due to the way the bone in his right thigh was broken.

Monitoring him periodically from elementary to Jr. High School, he never changed his mind about becoming a doctor. In high school he did well academically. He graduated in the top ten highest Academic Achievers with a 4.0 GPA in 1992. He attended Northeast University and completed his four years with a degree in Biology followed by a Master's Degree in Biology. He started prepping for his MCAT to enter medical school. Kevin applied to several schools of medicine. I was praying, knowing that he would receive mail for acceptance to medical school at LSU School of Medicine in New Orleans, LA. He said mom I will go to medical school in our home state, and it happened. Kevin was accepted to medical school at LSU School of Medicine in New Orleans, LA. He said mom I will go to medical school for four years and I will finish in four years. In August 2000, Kevin packed his bags and left for medical school. He had never spent any significant amount of time from home until medical school. He graduated from LSU School of Medicine in 2004. He entered Tulane Residential Program, wherein he did numerous procedures in the scope of his first year through the entire four and a half years. He chose Anesthesiology and graduated from Tulane Residential Program. He passed the Anesthesia Board Exam. Now he and his family live in Birmingham,

Alabama wherein he was accepted in a Fellowship Program in Critical Care Intensive Care Unit/ Anesthesiology. Kevin now is a father of one and also a husband. His wife is also attending Physician in the Emergency Room in Psychiatrics.

There wouldn't be any way for my children to have made the choices they made to live a structured and discipline life without God's help and guidance. I wasn't a perfect parent. I had to deal with myself as a woman, being provider for my family.

Planning and solving problems in the home in the midst of many challenges, I had to stay focused, strategize and planned to meet the needs of my children and myself. I look back and see how welfare was the open door to unlimited opportunities of being gainfully employed: The three steps are:

- . Step on welfare, financially deprived.
- . Step up while on welfare.
- . Step off welfare and give back.

I have been empowered by opened doors and avenues that can enhance and change the lives of women and children all because I made the Welfare System my stepping stone to a better life. June 2004, I retired from my nursing career with the state of Louisiana with 30 years in Pediatric Nursing, Adult PT Care, Psyche & Detox Unit, Ambulatory Care of Medicines, Diabetic Foot Care—Certified Podiatry. I'm involved in Ministry Outreach to the homeless and less fortunate. My nursing career continues in the form of short lectures, referrals to Medicaid community care facilities, encouraging health care for young people, immunizations, individuals who have been diagnosed with diabetes, hypertension, thyroid disease, women's health for annual pap smears, mammograms, men's health—referral for annual Prostate PSA, substance abuse, referral for transitional housing. I conduct workshops for girls and boys covering drugs and alcohol, juveniles and teen pregnancies. I'm consistently encouraging completing high school by getting their GED and further their education by getting involved in Tech and Vocational Schooling and colleges to develop what's on the inside of them to make a better life and obtain the necessary skills. It's not how you start but how you finish!

Today, This Is My Life

Look at where my Savior and Lord has brought me as a senior citizen at the age of 67. My four wonderful children are adults with their own families and my family is increasing with grandchildren and great-grandchildren. I think what a blessing to watch my children grown up, setting goals, working and being involved in their different careers. Yet I realized that God saw me through the gateway of purpose. God knew me before the foundation of the world, who and where I would go, decisions I would make, mistakes, problems, circumstances in my life and my relationship with Him. Time spent listening to the negative opinions that others expressed about me from childhood to adult. I got married at the age of 23, divorced from a spouse with a very lengthy drug habit. I received welfare for 18 months, the effects of the drug life on me and my children. All the time God was moving in my life. I began to see the picture clear after I was born again, victorious, got proper teaching of the Word of God. My mind was renewed by consistently reading and meditating on the spiritual principles as it plainly relates to every aspect of my life and my children's lives as well. God was after purpose for my life as He had originally planned. He never looked at the things I experienced. He only saw me through the gateway of purpose. God was after the deposits He had put into my life with purpose, to minister hope to many single women whose lives are shipped wrecked and limiting themselves on public welfare to single and married women who are in and out of relationships with a spouse and father who did not want to be committed to a family structure.

I am so truly thankful that I took what the Welfare System had to offer me in the way of childcare and education which opened the door to my nursing career which started in 1972 to this current day. I retired 6 years ago. My nursing career continues as I am a mom to many children and adult males and females needing referrals to resources available for healthcare and substance abuse and many others. My experience was very challenging as total support for my children due to abandonment of my ex-spouse. It was a very challenging one but God empowered me to do the job as a single parent. It wasn't based on what he did not do but on my responsibility as I was left in the situation with four children that were innocent. I was able to take care of my children and we managed to live above the beggarly element, the destroying and decaying perils of a family perishing because of it being depleted of finances to obtain the necessities of daily living. Because of the scope of my training as a nurse, I was able to do extended shifts of work to generate extra income to take care of my children. The way was made as I was blessed with all spiritual blessings: (Ephesians 1:3); inherited eternal life; observing and obeying the Lord's commandments (Deut. 28:12); doing all things through Christ who strengthens me (Phil. 4:13); strong in the Lord and in the power of His might (Ephesians 6:10); casting all my cares upon Jesus (I Peter 5:7).

Identified With The Word Of God

. A child of God (Romans 8:16)

. An heir of God and joint heir with Jesus (Romans 8:16)

. More than a conqueror (Romans 8:17)

. A laborer together with God (I Cor. 3:9)

. Being transformed by the renewing of your mind (Romans 12:1-2)

. The light of the world (Matthew 5:14)

. Crucified with Christ, nevertheless I live, yet not I, but Christ lives in me (Gal. 2:20)

. Walk by faith, not by sight (II Cor. 5:7)

. The righteousness of God in Christ (II Cor. 5:21)

. Bringing every thought into captivity (II Cor. 10:5)

. Casting down vain imaginations (II Cor. 4:4-5)

. Not moved by what I see (II Cor. 4:18)

. An overcomer by the blood of the lamb and the word of my testimony (Rev. 12:11)

. God's workmanship (Eph. 2:10)

. Establish God's Word here on earth (Matt. 16:19)

. Above only and not beneath (Deut. 28:13)

. My authority over the enemy (Luke 10:19)

. Healed by the stripes of Jesus (I Peter 2:24)

. Blessed with all spiritual blessings (Eph. 1:3)

. A new Creation in Christ (II Cor. 5:17)

. Observing and obeying the Lord's commandments (Deut. 28:12)

www.ingramcontent.com/pod-product-compliance
Lightning Source LLC
LaVergne TN
LVHW040201080526
838202LV00042B/3275